A TRUE BOOK™

The Seven Continents
Africa

ZUKISWA WANNER

Children's Press®
An Imprint of Scholastic Inc.

Content Consultant
Clemente Abrokwaa, Ph.D.,
Associate Teaching Professor of African Studies,
Penn State University

Library of Congress Cataloging-in-Publication Data
Names: Wanner, Zukiswa, author.
Title: Africa / by Zukiswa Wanner.
Description: New York, NY : Children's Press, an imprint of Scholastic Inc., 2019. | Series: A true book |
    Includes index.
Identifiers: LCCN 2018028749| ISBN 9780531128046 (library binding) | ISBN 9780531134122 (pbk.)
Subjects: LCSH: Africa—Juvenile literature.
Classification: LCC DT22 .W35 2019 | DDC 960—dc23
LC record available at https://lccn.loc.gov/2018028749

All rights reserved. Published in 2019 by Children's Press, an imprint of Scholastic Inc.
Printed in North Mankato, MN, USA 113

SCHOLASTIC, CHILDREN'S PRESS, A TRUE BOOK™, and associated logos are trademarks and/or
registered trademarks of Scholastic Inc.

Scholastic Inc., 557 Broadway, New York, NY 10012

4 5 6 7 8 9 10 R 28 27 26 25 24 23 22 21

Front: Africa
Back: Children in Uganda

Find the Truth!

Everything you are about to read is true *except* for one of the sentences on this page.

Which one is **TRUE**?

T or F The Sahara Desert was once full of farmland.

T or F The weather throughout most of Africa is cold year-round.

Find the answers in this book.

Contents

Map: Continent Close-up **6**

1 Land and Climate

What's the terrain of Africa like, and
what are its usual weather conditions? **9**

2 Plants and Animals

What communities of living things
make their homes in Africa? **17**

THE BIG TRUTH!

Electronic Waste

How are old electronics affecting
life for people in Africa? **24**

Lion

Workers harvest tea leaves

3 A Peek at the Past

How has Africa changed over time?. **27**

4 Africa Today

What is life like for people in Africa? **35**

Destination: Africa **42**

True Statistics:

Continental Extremes. **44**

Resources **45**

Important Words. **46**

Index **47**

About the Author. **48**

African elephant

EUROPE

Strait of Gibraltar

Canary Islands
(Spain)

Western
Sahara
(disputed
territory)

MOROCCO

TUNISIA

Mediterranean Sea

Suez Canal

N
W   E
S

ASIA

ALGERIA

LIBYA

EGYPT

Cairo

SENEGAL

MAURITANIA

MALI

Niger River

NIGER

CHAD

SUDAN

Nile River

Red Sea

ERITREA

DJIBOUTI

GAMBIA

GUINEA

BURKINA
FASO

Lake Chad

NIGERIA
Abuja

SOMALIA

GUINEA-
BISSAU

CÔTE
D'IVOIRE

CAMEROON

CENTRAL AFR. REP.

SOUTH
SUDAN

Addis Ababa
ETHIOPIA

SIERRA
LEONE   LIBERIA

GHANA

TOGO

BENIN

Congo River

UGANDA

KENYA

Equator

Gulf of
Guinea

GABON

RWANDA

L. Victoria

INDIA
OCEA

Equat

SÃO TOMÉ & PRÍNCIPE
EQUITORIAL GUINEA

DEM. REP.
OF THE
CONGO

BURUNDI

CABO VERDE

Inset

REPUBLIC
OF THE
CONGO

Kinshasa

TANZANIA

Zanzibar

COMOROS

100 mi West
of Gambia

ANGOLA

ZAMBIA

Zambezi R.

MALAWI

MOZAMBIQUE

ZIMBABWE

MADAGASCAR

ATLANTIC
OCEAN

NAMIBIA

BOTSWANA

Pretoria

ESWATINI
(SWAZILAND)

LESOTHO

SEYCHE

Inset

0   600 MI

0   1,000 KM

SOUTH
AFRICA

Cape of
Good Hope

MADAGASCAR

MAUR

Réunion
(France)

Continent Close-up

As the second-largest of

Egypt

Earth's seven continents, Africa is home to a dazzling array of cultures. Its mainland is surrounded by the Atlantic Ocean to the west, the Mediterranean Sea to the north, the Red Sea to the northeast, and the Indian Ocean to the east. The continent also has many islands. In the Atlantic Ocean are São Tomé and Príncipe as well as Cape Verde. Madagascar, Seychelles, Comoros, and Mauritius lie in the Indian Ocean.

Land area	11,724,000 square miles (30,365,021 square kilometers)
Number of countries	55
Estimated population (2016)	1.216 billion
Main languages	Arabic, Swahili, Hausa, and between 1,000 and 2,000 other languages
Largest country	Algeria
Smallest country	Seychelles
Fast fact	There are about 170 million Facebook users in Africa.

Lake Victoria

Ngorongoro Conservation Area is located in the crater of a huge volcano!

Tanzania's Ngorongoro Conservation Area is home to an incredible range of wildlife.

CHAPTER 1

Land and Climate

From vast deserts and towering mountain peaks to bustling cities, Africa contains a beautiful and varied landscape. The highest parts of the continent lie in Southern and East Africa, while West and North Africa are flatter. Most of the highlands and mountains in East Africa are a result of volcanic activity. Africa's coastline is straighter and smoother compared to most other continents. It has fewer bays and other inlets. As a result, it has fewer natural harbors.

A Tropical Continent

Most of Africa lies between the **tropics** of Capricorn and Cancer. This means the continent mostly falls within the tropical zone. This is the part of Earth that lies closest to the sun.

Africa is almost equally divided in half by the **equator**. São Tomé and Príncipe, Gabon, the Republic of the Congo, the Democratic Republic of the Congo, Uganda, Kenya, and Somalia all lie along the equator. The continent's other nations fall to the north or the south of this line.

Mozambique's Quirimbas Islands are among the many small landmasses along Africa's coast.

Rushing Rivers

Several waterways crisscross the continent. The longest of them, at 4,258 miles (6,853 km), is the Nile River. The river's source is often disputed by two neighboring countries, Rwanda and Uganda. Both claim the river begins within their borders. Other major rivers include the Congo in central Africa, which is 2,920 miles (4,700 km) long. The Niger River in West Africa stretches for 2,597 miles (4,180 km) and empties into the Atlantic Ocean.

Tropic of Cancer

Atlas Mtns.

Tademait Plateau

Ethiopian Highlands

Great Rift Valley

Equator

Mt. Kilimanjaro

INDIAN OCEAN

KEY

TERRAIN

Mountains   Hills   Lowlands

Bie Plateau

Tropic of Capricorn

ATLANTIC OCEAN

Drakensberg Mtns.

This map shows where Africa's higher and lower areas are.

Large Lakes

Among Africa's greatest lakes are Lakes Volta, Victoria, and Malawi. Lake Volta is in Ghana. It is the world's largest human-made lake. Lakes Victoria and Malawi both lie on the Great Rift Valley in East Africa. Lake Malawi is also called Lake Nyasa. When Scottish explorer David Livingstone asked one of his African guides what the lake was called, the guide answered, "*nyasa*." Livingstone then named it Lake Nyasa, not knowing that nyasa simply means "lake" in the Bantu languages that are spoken in Malawi.

Lake Victoria contains hundreds of different kinds of fish.

Many parts of Africa go through long rainy seasons followed by periods of little to no rain at all.

RECORD TEMPERATURES

HIGHEST	LOWEST
Kebili, Tunisia; July 7, 1931	Ifrane, Morocco; February 11, 1935
131°F	−11.2°F
55°C	−24°C

Water and Weather

Large bodies of water such as oceans and lakes can help keep weather in the surrounding areas from becoming too extreme. In Africa's interior, these large bodies of water are few and far between. As a result, temperatures can get very warm in summer or during the day and very cold in winter or at night. Temperatures are highest in the Sahara Desert and lowest across the south and atop mountains.

With a height of 19,341 feet (5,895 m), Tanzania's Mount Kilimanjaro is the tallest peak in all of Africa.

Hot and Cold

Some parts of Africa are very hot year-round. For example, in Dallol, Ethiopia, the average temperature throughout the year is about 91 degrees Fahrenheit (33 degrees Celsius). In other parts of the continent, the weather is less extreme. Snow regularly falls in the Atlas Mountains and on Mount Kilimanjaro. There are also **glaciers** on the Rwenzori Mountains at the border of Uganda and the Democratic Republic of the Congo. However, they are now under threat due to global **climate change**.

Victoria Falls

Victoria Falls is known in the local Tonga language as *Mosi-oa-Tunya*, which means "the smoke that thunders." It is a waterfall in southern Africa on the Zambezi River, between Zambia and Zimbabwe. It is considered the world's largest waterfall based on its width of 5,604 feet (1,708 meters) and height of 354 feet (108 m). These dimensions result in an amazingly enormous sheet of falling water. Victoria Falls has been selected as a United Nations World Heritage Site.

Victoria Falls is more than twice as tall as the famous Niagara Falls in North America.

An African elephant's trunk contains about 100,000 different muscles!

African elephants are Earth's largest land animals.

CHAPTER 2

Plants and Animals

Africa has several major physical regions. They include the Sahel, the Ethiopian Highlands, the African Great Lakes, the Swahili Coast, southern Africa, and the Sahara Desert. These regions all host distinctive biomes. A biome is a large geographical area where certain plant and animal species live. These species are all suited to thrive in the biome's climate and geography.

Regional Differences

Biomes can spread across different regions. For example, in the Sahel area of northern Africa, there are savanna and desert areas. The mountainous Ethiopian Highlands lie within a savanna biome. The African Great Lakes contain freshwater biomes surrounded by savanna. The Swahili Coast covers the eastern seaboard of Africa. It is part of a savanna biome.

Geladas are monkeys that are found only in the mountains of Ethiopia.

In Morocco, goats climb high into the branches of argan trees to eat fruit.

Differing Climates

An area's climate plays a role in what kind of biome it has. For example, the Mediterranean climate is defined by mild, wet winters and warm, dry summers. This kind of climate is experienced by northern African countries such as Morocco and coastal Tunisia. Another Mediterranean climate zone is in the Western Cape in South Africa. The weather in these places is perfect for plant eaters such as goats and sheep. Other animals, such as jackals and lynxes, hunt the plant-eating species.

Equator

ATLANTIC
OCEAN

BIOMES

- Rain forest
- Temperate forest
- Desert
- Savanna
- Fresh water

INDIAN
OCEAN

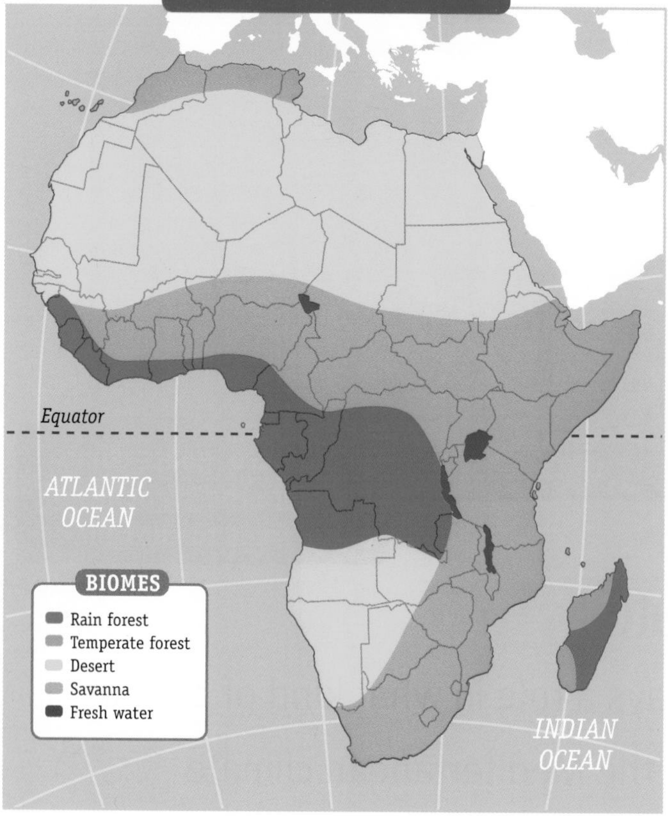

Deep in the Rain Forest

Most of Africa's native rain forests have been destroyed by development, agriculture, and forestry. But the remaining rain forests have a rich variety of animal life. For example, a patch of rain forest measuring 2.3 square miles (6 sq km) could contain up to 400 bird species, 150 butterfly species, and 60 species of amphibians. Africa's rain forest mammals include African forest elephants, gorillas, and the okapi, a donkey-like giraffe.

The Savanna

Wide-open grasslands called savannas cover almost half of Africa. Among the continent's many savanna regions, the Serengeti is the most well-known. It is a vast, rolling plain that stretches 11,583 square miles (30,000 sq km) from Kenya's Masai-Mara National Reserve to Tanzania's Serengeti National Park. The Serengeti is home to an incredible variety of animals, including wildebeests, lions, elephants, cheetahs, zebras, and giraffes.

There are more than 5 million square miles (13 million sq km) of savanna in Africa.

Hot, Dry, and Dusty Deserts

There are several deserts in Africa, including the Kalahari, the Namib, and the Sahara. The Sahara is the world's largest hot desert, covering 3.3 million square miles (8.5 million sq km) of land. Defining Africa's northern bulge, the Sahara makes up 25 percent of the continent. Horned vipers, golden jackals, ostriches, and fennec foxes are just some of the animals that can be found there.

The Berber people of North Africa have traditionally relied on camels to travel through deserts.

Species in Trouble

Many of Africa's plant and animal species are in danger of dying out, often due to human activities. Here are just a few:

Ethiopian Wolf

Home: Ethiopia

Farmland has grown to cover much of this wolf's natural habitat. This has forced Ethiopian wolves to move to higher and higher areas.

African Elephant

Home: Areas south of the Sahara Desert

Because some people are willing to pay a high price for ivory, many elephants are killed for their tusks. This trade is illegal today, but it has not completely stopped. As a result, some African elephant populations remain endangered.

Cheetah

Home: Southern, northern, and eastern Africa

Cheetahs live in large open areas. But as our world grows and the human population increases, these big cats are left with less space to hunt.

Mountain Gorilla

Home: Uganda, Rwanda, the Democratic Republic of Congo

Due to **poaching** and violent wars between groups of local people, the mountain gorilla has become the most endangered type of gorilla in the world.

Pygmy Hippopotamus

Home: West Africa

There are fewer than 2,000 pygmy hippos left in the wild. Their numbers are declining as their habitat is destroyed and they continue to be hunted for meat.

Lion

Home: Areas south of the Sahara Desert

Lions face many threats, including habitat loss. Local people kill these cats to protect their livestock, while rich tourists visit Africa to hunt lions in the wild.

Electronic Waste

New and improved versions of the latest computers, phones, video game systems, and other electronics are constantly being released. Many people around the world throw out their electronics as soon as newer, shinier models become available. As a result, millions of tons of "e-waste" are created every year.

E-waste from around the world often ends up illegally dumped in African countries. These countries have little experience dealing with e-waste and lack the equipment to dispose of it properly. As a result, they have difficulty managing the mounds of trash. This can lead to major environmental and economic problems. The next page explains a few of them.

LAPTOPS

MICROWAVES

HOUSEHOLD APPLIANCES

ELECTRIC SHAVERS

WASHING MACHINES

TVS

TABLETS

COMPUTERS

DANGEROUS WORK

People are paid to sift through the landfills and sort out different types of items. However, these workers are not given proper protection.

POLLUTED WATER

There is serious concern that people's blood might be absorbing lead from the electronics. Additionally, the e-waste causes pollution in nearby waterways. When people or animals eat fish from these waterways, they consume the pollution as well.

PILING UP

The West African nation of Ghana is one of the countries that has been hit hardest by the consequences of e-waste. Agbogbloshie, an area in the capital city of Accra, is one of the most concentrated e-waste sites in the world. Here, massive landfills are piled high with electronics that have been discarded over the years.

ELECTRIC TOOLS

PHONES

In 1959, in Olduvai Gorge, archaeologists Richard and Mary Leakey identified remains of what were at the time the world's earliest known human ancestors.

The Olduvai Gorge in Tanzania has been the location of many important discoveries about the early history of humans.

A Peek at the Past

The earliest known humans lived in Africa. Historians believe that some **hominids** began to leave Africa and spread to the Middle East and Asia 1.4 million years ago and to Europe a million years ago. Those that stayed and those that left are the ancestors of all of today's humans. As a result, Africa is often called the Cradle of Humankind.

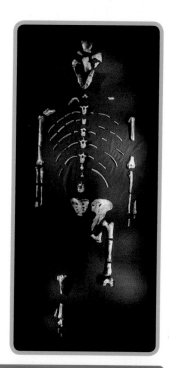

The fossilized skeleton of Lucy, the most complete discovery of an ancient hominid, is about 3.2 million years old. Lucy was discovered in Ethiopia's Great Rift Valley.

Algeria's Tassili n'Ajjer region contains about 15,000 cave drawings that date back thousands of years.

Prehistory

African prehistory reaches back at least 2.5 million years, when the first tool-making hominids appeared on the continent. Over time, they developed into modern humans. The Nile Valley was a favored location for early hunter-gatherer societies. The Sahara also drew early people. The region was wetter than it is today and supported wide areas of fertile grassland and many shallow lakes. By about 7000 BCE, Africa's people had begun farming, raising livestock, and building permanent settlements.

Ancient Egypt

Beginning in the 3000s BCE, the ancient Egyptian civilization flourished in the Nile Valley. Egyptians grew grain and other crops in the rich soil near the Nile. They were also master builders. Some of the huge stone pyramids they constructed thousands of years ago still stand today. Egypt's writing systems, called hieroglyphs and hieratic script, were among the first ever created.

The modern English alphabet was likely based on ancient Egyptian hieroglyphs when it was created.

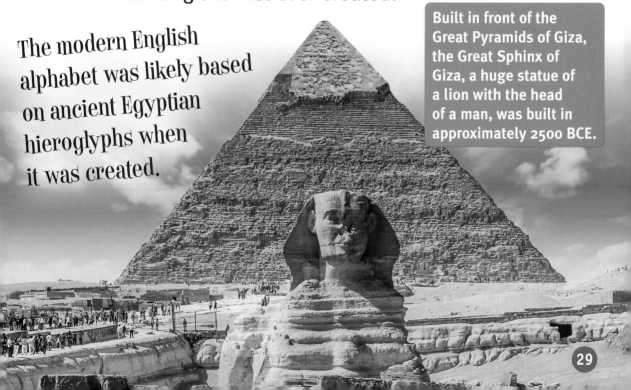

Built in front of the Great Pyramids of Giza, the Great Sphinx of Giza, a huge statue of a lion with the head of a man, was built in approximately 2500 BCE.

Spreading Across the Continent

The Sahara started drying slowly about 6,000 years ago. This pushed many people southward to the West African savanna and the East African highlands by about 2000 BCE.

In the seventh century CE, Arab soldiers entered Africa through Egypt. They spread their religion, Islam, to cities such as Cairo and Alexandria. It has been a major religion in Africa ever since.

Timeline of African History

3000
Ancient Egyptians develop some of the world's first forms of writing.

859 CE
The University of Karueei the first African university is founded in Fez, Morocc by Fatima al-Fihri. Today, it is the oldest operating university in the world.

| 7000 BCE | 3000 | 2630 | 859 CE |

7000 BCE
African people begin farming for the first time.

2630
The earliest known pyramid in Egypt, the Pyramid of Djoser, is built.

The Transatlantic Slave Trade

The first known European to reach Africa was Portugal's Bartholomew Dias in 1488. The arrival of the Europeans began the tragic era of the transatlantic slave trade. During this time, European traders came to the continent and purchased millions of enslaved Africans from Arab and African traders. The traders then sold their slaves to plantation owners in North and South America.

1884
The Berlin Conference results in Europeans splitting up Africa for **colonization**.

1994
Following the end of apartheid, Nelson Mandela becomes the first democratically elected president of South Africa.

| 16th–19th centuries | 1884 | 1948 | 1994 |

16th–19th centuries
During the transatlantic slave trade, 10 million to 12 million Africans are forced into slavery and shipped to the Americas.

1948
Apartheid, a formal system of discrimination against black people, begins in South Africa.

31

The Era of Colonization

Europeans did not enter the African interior until the 1800s. Among the first to travel into Africa was the English explorer Henry Morton Stanley. Stanley and his fellow Europeans' visits to the continent led to the Berlin Conference. This 1884 arrangement between the major European nations divided Africa into colonies. Only Ethiopia and Liberia were not colonized. In 1957, under the leadership of Kwame Nkrumah, Ghana became the first country south of the Sahara Desert to gain independence from Europe. Others soon followed.

Henry Morton Stanley poses with an African guide during one of his visits to the continent.

This rock art is an important primary source for researchers who want to study the San people.

San Rock Art

One way scholars have learned about African history is by studying rock art created by the San people of southern Africa. Found in caves, the rock art is believed to have been drawn from the 2000s BCE until the 1800s CE. Rock art was not only artistic expression. It was also used to pass messages to future cave dwellers in eastern and southern Africa. In the Drakensberg mountain range of South Africa alone, there are more than 35,000 images spread across 600 sites.

The streets of busy cities such as Lagos, Nigeria, are often crowded with cars and people.

Africa's people make up almost 17 percent of the world's total population.

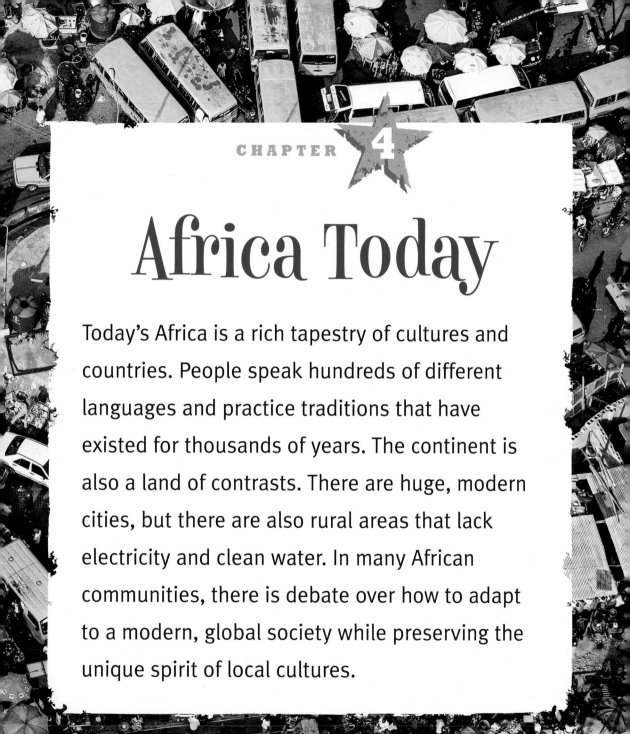

CHAPTER 4

Africa Today

Today's Africa is a rich tapestry of cultures and countries. People speak hundreds of different languages and practice traditions that have existed for thousands of years. The continent is also a land of contrasts. There are huge, modern cities, but there are also rural areas that lack electricity and clean water. In many African communities, there is debate over how to adapt to a modern, global society while preserving the unique spirit of local cultures.

Strength and Progress

Throughout the 20th century, civil wars, poverty, and disease were major problems in much of Africa. Today, African governments are more involved in peacekeeping efforts. There is also greater cooperation between countries to fight diseases such as Ebola and HIV/AIDS. Another positive change is that the continent's children, especially its girls, have access to better education systems.

Ugandan school children play in their village near the city of Lira.

The African Union works to promote peace and cooperation among the countries of Africa.

The 55 nations of Africa are all members of a larger group called the African Union.

African Governments

Many African governments are republics. This means government leaders are elected by the people. Almost all of the countries hold general elections every four or five years. The exceptions are Gabon, which has elections after six years, and Senegal, which gives its leaders seven years in power.

The Kingdoms of Morocco and eSwatini (Swaziland) are constitutional monarchies. This means they have kings, but their people elect representatives to the **legislature**.

Workers harvest tea leaves on a farm in Rwanda.

African Agriculture

Farming is an essential part of life for many Africans. About 60 percent of the continent's people survive by growing their own food. Wheat, barley, and grapes are commonly farmed on Africa's Mediterranean coast. Date palms, fig trees, and cotton are grown in the **oases** of the desert. East and southern Africans grow crops such as cotton, coffee, and tea. They also keep goats, camels, sheep, and cattle as domestic animals.

Made in Africa

An export is a product that a country sells to other nations. African countries make most of their money through the export of minerals and agricultural products. Africa's many valuable natural resources include oil, diamonds, gold, and platinum. Crops such as cotton, timber, cacao, and coffee are grown for export. Service and manufacturing industries are also on the rise in many countries.

This graph shows the top export for each of Africa's four top exporting countries.

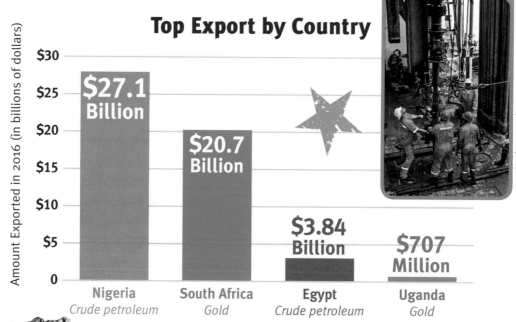

Top Export by Country

Amount Exported in 2016 (in billions of dollars)

Country	Amount
Nigeria *Crude petroleum*	**$27.1 Billion**
South Africa *Gold*	**$20.7 Billion**
Egypt *Crude petroleum*	**$3.84 Billion**
Uganda *Gold*	**$707 Million**

Source: MIT Observatory of Economic Complexity

Fun and Food

The biggest sports in Africa are soccer, netball, boxing, and rugby. Since 1957, African countries have competed in a continent-wide soccer competition called the Africa Cup of Nations (AFCON).

People across Africa enjoy a wide range of local cuisines. Northern African food has a strong Arab influence. Stews and soups are popular across the continent. *Fufu* is a soft, starchy food made from plantains and cassava that is beloved in central and West Africa. In Ethiopia, thin bread called *injera* is a staple.

Soccer is a popular activity throughout all of Africa.

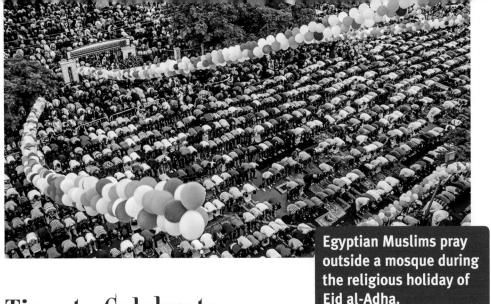

Egyptian Muslims pray outside a mosque during the religious holiday of Eid al-Adha.

Time to Celebrate

The nations of Africa enjoy a variety of exciting holidays and traditions. Religious holidays such as Islam's Eid al-Fitr and Christianity's Christmas are celebrated across much of the continent. Many countries also observe National Days to celebrate the anniversaries of their independence from colonial powers.

Africa is a vast and vibrant continent. With its rich, diverse culture and remarkable contributions to history, it has made an unmistakable mark on our world. ★

Destination: Africa

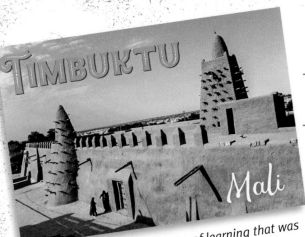

TIMBUKTU — Mali

Timbuktu was a thriving center of learning that was instrumental in the spread of Islam in Africa. It was the capital of the Mali and Songhai empires. Today, it retains three notable mosques and one of the world's great collections of ancient manuscripts.

THE HOUSE OF SLAVES (MAISON DES ESCLAVES) — Senegal

The House of Slaves and its Door of No Return is a museum and memorial to the transatlantic slave trade on Gorée Island. The museum, which opened in 1962, memorializes the final exit point of slaves from Africa.

THE PYRAMIDS OF GIZA AND THE SPHINX — Egypt

This complex contains several of the most impressive ancient Egyptian pyramids as well as the Great Sphinx, a statue of a mythical creature with the body of a lion and the head of a human. (Check out a photo of the sphinx on page 29!)

THE WILDEBEEST MIGRATION

Tanzania and Kenya

Each year, more than a million wildebeests, zebras, and antelopes migrate clockwise around the Serengeti-Masai Mara area during the famous Wildebeest Migration. The animals travel between Tanzania and Kenya, stopping along the way to give birth. It is one of the world's most spectacular natural events.

VICTORIA FALLS

Zambia and Zimbabwe

Victoria Falls is located on the Zambezi River between Zambia and Zimbabwe. It is the world's largest waterfall.

TABLE MOUNTAIN

South Africa

Table Mountain is a flat-topped mountain overlooking the city of Cape Town, South Africa. It is a major tourist attraction, and many visitors like to hike to the top.

GREAT ZIMBABWE

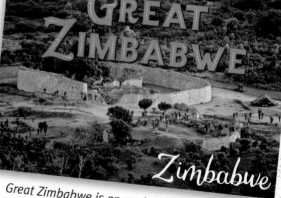

Zimbabwe

Great Zimbabwe is an ancient city in southeast Zimbabwe. The stone walls, some of which were over 16.5 feet (5 m) high, were constructed hundreds of years ago without cement, but the structures have never fallen.

Number of mobile phone users in Africa: About 500 million

Number of mammal species in Africa: More than 1,100

Number of bird species in Africa: More than 2,600

Top speed of a cheetah: 70 mph (112.6 kph)

Population of Cairo, Egypt, Africa's largest urban area: 15.6 million

Highest elevation: Mount Kilimanjaro: 19,341 feet (5,895 m)

Average population density of Africa: 33 people per square mile (87 people per sq km)

Did you find the truth?

T The Sahara Desert was once full of farmland.

F The weather throughout most of Africa is cold year-round.

Resources

Books

Bjorklund, Ruth. *Liberia*. New York: Children's Press, 2016.

Burgan, Michael. *Kenya*. New York: Children's Press, 2015.

Hintz, Martin. *Algeria*. New York: Children's Press, 2017.

Rogers Seavey, Lura. *Nigeria*. New York: Children's Press, 2017.

Somervill, Barbara A. *Niger*. New York: Children's Press, 2017.

Williams, Rachel. *Atlas of Adventures*. New York: Wide Eyed Editions, 2015.

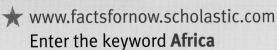

Visit this Scholastic website for more information on Africa:

⭐ www.factsfornow.scholastic.com
Enter the keyword **Africa**

Important Words

climate change (KLYE-mit CHAYNJ) global warming and other changes in the weather that are happening because of human activity

colonization (kah-luh-nih-ZAY-shun) a system where land is taken over and controlled by a foreign country

equator (ih-KWAY-tur) an imaginary line around the middle of Earth that is an equal distance from the North and South Poles

glaciers (GLAY-shurz) slow-moving masses of ice found in mountain valleys or polar regions

hominids (HAH-muh-nidz) a family of mammals that includes humans, apes, and their ancestors

legislature (LEJ-is-lay-chur) a group of people who have the power to make or change laws for a country or state

oases (oh-AY-sees) places in the desert where water can be found above the ground and where plants and trees can grow

poaching (POH-ching) the practice of hunting or fishing illegally

tropics (TRAH-piks) the two parallel latitudes that are a specific distance north or south of the equator where the sun is directly overhead in the sky

Index

Page numbers in **bold** indicate illustrations.

animals, **8–9**, **16–17**, **18**, **19**, **20**, **21**, **22**, **23**, 28, 38, **43**
apartheid, 31
art, **28**, **33**

birds, 20

camels, **22**, 38
climate, **13**, 14, 19

desert biomes, 13, 18, **22**, 30, 38
diseases, 36

early people, **28**, **33**
economy, 24, **39**
education, 30, **36**
Egyptian civilization, **29**, **30**, **42**
elephants, **16–17**, 20, 21, **23**
elevation, **14**
European colonization, 31, 32, 41
exports, **39**

farming, 20, 28, 29, 30, **38**, 39
fish, **12**, 25
foods, 38, 40
fossils, **26**, **27**

goats, **19**, 38
governments, 31, 36, **37**

holidays, **41**
hominids, **26**, 27, 28

islands, 7, **10**, **42**

lakes, **12**, 13, 18, 28

land area, 7
landscape, 9, 18, **26–27**, **43**
languages, 7, 12, 15, 29, 30, 35

Mandela, Nelson, 31
maps, **6**, **11**, **19**
mining, 39
mountains, 9, 13, **14**, **18**, 33, **43**

national parks, 21
Nkrumah, Kwame, 32

oceans, 7, 11, 13

pollution, **24–25**
population, 7, 23, **34–35**

rain forest biomes, 18, 19
religion, 30, **41**, 42
rivers, **11**, 15, 43

savanna biomes, 18, **21**, 28
seas, 7
slavery, **31**, **42**
sports, **40**

timeline, **30–31**
tourism, **11**, 23, 43

Victoria Falls, **15**, **43**
volcanoes, 9

wildebeests, 21, **43**

zebras, **21**, 43

About the Author

Zukiswa Wanner is the author of four novels, two works of nonfiction, and two children's books. In 2014, Wanner was selected by Hay Festival as one of 39 African writers most likely to change the face of literature in sub-Saharan Africa. She is a curator of Artistic Encounters in Nairobi, Kenya, and recently founded a publishing house, Paivapo, which seeks to create a more intimate conversation between African writers and readers through translation of works in the continent's different languages.